Random Writings

AF624667

Michelle Handyside

BookLeaf Publishing

Presentation by *BookLeaf Publishing*

Web: www.bookleafpub.com

E-mail: info@bookleafpub.com

ISBN: 978-93-95784-43-6

First edition 2022

DEDICATION

To all those who have helped me along my path. To those who cheered and those who jeered and those who taught me who I truly am.

ACKNOWLEDGEMENT

This book wouldn't exist without the encouragement and support of my best friend and my own Prince among men Mark Handyside. You always said I could do it and now I have.

Cold

Snow crunches underfoot,
Wild wind blows cold.
I pull my scarf closer to try and be warm,
As I walk away from you.

Winter makes the colours sleep,
It's white, grey and monotone.
Each step is hard to stay on my feet,
And I wend my weary way home,

Turn on the light, turn on the fire,
Put on the kettle once more.
Don't look in the mirror to see my face,
I try to start over once again.
It's so cold.

Music

Drums, guitar, keyboard, bass put it all together
and you know what it makes, music.
Music.
Music that can make you dance, take a chance,
shed a tear or sing along.
All I need is a beat steady and strong.
For as long as I recall I listened to it all.
Plucky strings, heavy hits,folksy winds.
Music.
Music an armour, a teacher, a friend.
Sing along to words you gear again and again.
Not alone, but unique like the melodies I hear
All I need is music.

A Unicorn

I'm sure I saw a unicorn
When I was out walking today,
A long flowing mane,
Sparkling eyes,
Heading out on her own way.

She didn't hear me passing by,
She didn't see me or move at all.
I wondered what she was thinking,
As she stood beside the wall.

Unique, independent and magical,
Confident, strong and bold.
I saw a unicorn today
And Amy's only 13 years old.

At The Movies

Images flicker on the screen,
Of times to come and times that's been..
Historical tales, sci-fi, war, romance,
Sights to amaze, imagination run wild,
Some for the adult, some for the child.
The smell of the popcorn, salted or sweet.
Nachos or hotdogs or pick n mix sweet.
Grab your drink and take your seat.
The big screen is calling you into the dark
At the cinema.

Why?

Why are we always losing our tempers?
Why is it so easy to snipe?
Why do we like to see each other lose?
When we're supposed to be in love.

Why aren't you holding my hand anymore?
Why won't I sit by your side?
Why don't we kiss in the darkness now?
When we're supposed to be in love

Why does it seem like we're islands now?
Why do I feel so alone?
Why can't we push pride aside this time?
When we're supposed to be in love.

Why did you buy me these roses tonight?
Why are you offering me a ring?
Why is making up the best part of a fight?
As we finally know we're in love.

What Will I Be?

I remember as a little girl everyone asking me,
"Michelle, flower, what do you want to be?"
I had so many dreams back then each greater than the last.
It's strange the kind of answers I gave them in the past.

"I want to be a policewoman, that's what I want to be,
The one who just jailed the crooks, well that'll be me.
I'll drive the police car and have a police dog too,
A policewoman, yeah that's what I think I'm gonna do."

"I want to be a stunt girl, that's what I want to be,
Doing all the exciting stuff, well that'll be me.
Jumping off high buildings and flipping fast cars too.
A stunt girl, yeah I think that's what I'm gonna do."

"I want to be a film star, that's what I want to be,
The face on all the magazines, well that'll be me.
I'll make lots of money and kiss handsome actors too.
A film star, yeah I think that's what I'm gonna do."

"I want to be a nurse now, that's what I want to be,
The one giving out injections, well that'll be me.
I'll take care of all the patients and give out medicine too.
A nurse, yeah I think that's what I'm gonna do."

Time passes quickly and I grew as you can see,
A nurse was my career path that I follow happily.
I know what I should have answered then now though
"I'm just gonna be me."

The Long Road

My feet are so tired, they ache
The sun is burning my back.
Ahead I see the shimmering light of the moon,
So I walk on further.

Behind me further down the road,
Are the dreams and hopes I once had.
My innocence turned, twisted, mutated
Into bitter cynicism.

The people I once cared forget their Mark on
this path,
A broken plate, a warped stick of wood.
I cant look over twisted frame of bone,
Ahead the way is the last unknown.

The moonlight shows another traveller,
He walks the same path but we never speak.
I know the journey will be over soon,
The long road will reach its end.

The Candle

Candle flicker through the night,
Make the darkness dimly bright.
Burn steadily as each night before,
As I wait for him to come home to our door.

The winter nights cold damp and dark,
From the gentle fire I take a spark.
The candlelight shines as the wax drips,
Then I feel his soft velvet lips.

A kiss on my cheek to make me wake,
Soon the brightest dawn will break
He holds me close, he holds me tight,
As we love alone in the candles light.

One night the flame will not burn,
From his work my lover won't return.
The dangers can't be kept away for long,
After the candle's light has gone.

My Teddy Bear

My Teddy bear is yellow and white,
He sleeps with me every night.
I hold him in my arms so tight
After my daddy switches off my light.

My Teddy bear is as old as me,
He's my best friend as anyone can see.
I share with him a birthday tea
Under the shade of my favourite tree.

My Teddy bears legs don't bend,
And there are a few holes Mommy needs to
mend.
But he's always been my favourite friend,
And our friendship will never end.

Games

One or two, three or four
As the dice rolls on the floor.
Throw a five or a six
And pick up that many sticks.
Throw a ball in the air
Call out the colour of someone's hair,
That person the ball must catch
But Suzy play properly, now don't you snatch.
Games to play in the playground
Instead of running around.
Games teach you how to add or share
Childhood days without a care.

A Child's Prayer

Kneeling by the bed with my eyes shut tight,
I pray to you God watch over me tonight.
I know I'm sometimes bad, but most the time I'm good,
And there's a few things I'd like if you could...

Mammy takes care of me, cooks, cleans and sews,
So for my Mammy I ask you give her some new clothes.
Daddy's always working, at meetings or online,
So for my Daddy please give him more time.

Then we come to me, the last one on the list,
All I ask for myself is for the teddy bear I kissed,
I hugged him in the shop and I've loved him for so long.
I always go to visit incase he might be gone.

So please listen God, to my prayer on this night,
Whatever I do wrong, I'll try to make it right,
Please bless the other children and let there be peace too.
I say Amen, climb into bed and oh yes, bless you too.

The Cove

I remember the waves slapping the rocks
And the way light glistened on the sea.
The sun was slowly setting on the horizon that night
We spent the night in the cove, you and me.

It was late summer, I'd just finished school
Life was an open book for me.
We sat on the beach for days at a time
In our little cove close to the sea.

We then separated, went back to life alone
Uncertain of what our futures would hold.
I married a good man, you moved to the coast
And like the cove we both became old.

I went back there today just to see it again
I heard the waves crash and birds cry.
My husband left long ago. Now you've left me too
So alone in this cove my heart will die.

The Man Behind The Mask

The matches are long over
Crowds of cheering people are long gone.
All that's left as his company
Is the radio playing some old song.

A bright bulb shines to light the room,
He packs sweaty ring tights away.
He looks at the diary in his bag
Tomorrow he's in Santa Fe.

No one sees his head shaking
The loneliness he feels inside,
He's a wrestler, a hero to millions
But what's him, he's forced to hide.

He isn't a champion, he may never be
He looks from the window and all fans are gone
He's done his job for another night
Now all that's left is the radio playing that same
old song.

People say they'd love to be him
Fighting to entertain is such a simple task
Yet no one ever knows or truly cares for him
The man behind the invisible mask.

The Midnight Ride

She climbed upon her stallion's back,
Holding tightly to his mane tar black.
A hooded cloak obscured her face
As men and hounds began their chase.
The moon was high, the night was cold
A winter's night straight from the mould.
She spurred on the horse fast through the stream
Just as she had done in a distant dream.
The mens calls and the dog's howls combined,
She started to feel she was running out of time.
Suddenly she noticed the light on the hill
And in that instant hee pursuers seemed still.
The castle gates opened, she hurried inside
Reaching the end of her midnight ride.
She followed the servant into the hall
Removing her cloak she joined in the ball.
She laughed and she waltzed all through the night
To be in this company just felt so right.
When daylight broke and sun tinged the sky
She remounted her horse and away did she ride.
Each morning she left the castle just after dawn
As she rode to the stream she chased a young fawn.
She saw the stone men and their dogs' marbled hides
Victims of the Dark Lady's midnight ride.

Little Girl

I sat and watched my little girl at play
When it rained the other day
And watching her it brought back to me
The little girl I used to be.

She sat and plaited her dolly's hair
Then sat the baby in her little pushchair
Watching her it could've been me
The little girl I used to be.

Later she drew a palace where she wanted to live
With all the care and love she could give
I sat and drew my own, especially for me
And the little girl I used to be.

Darkness In The Moonlight

Being born was my irreparable curse,
A slave to this thing called living
Condemned to survive every situation,
I lost the war from the very beginning.

No warmth, no comfort, nowhere to hide
From the constant compulsion to exist
How many tortures must I endure
Before I'm finally pardoned and released.

Have you ever seen compassion in a strangers eyes
Felt understanding in their touch?
Lucky you for me there's not but hate
Revulsion, segregation, distrust.

Have you seen the wildness in a person's eyes
When the face of the Reaper they see
In the instant they're aware of their mortality
Their fear and incomprehension excites me.

The crimson chianti I taste on my lips
Removes the melancholic veil
Rejuvenated my passion rages again
On the current of terror I sail.

I've probably passed you on a dark winter night
Somewhere beneath a nightclub sign

Maybe talked about life beneath a blood red neon light
But if you don't remember, that's fine.

I saw your blood pumping, I felt your heart beat
Your desire to live was so strong
Yet as dawns rays started to fill the street
You suddenly noticed I'd gone.

I've read all the fiction written about our race
Been to the midnight movie shows too
But for all that you gain with your colourless face
You lose a lot more, yes you do.

I never can walk in a warm spring rain
With someone I love at my side.
Though you never die and aren't supposed to feel pain
I'd give it all to watch my child on a slide.'

I'm too human to belong in this empty dark world
But not human enough for the day
I wish I could just give the clock hands a turn
And from sunlight I never would stray.

You don't know what you have til you lose it
I've lost my whole world so I know
With a soul in torment you just sit
Waiting for every black day to go.

So why don't I end it I hear you all cry
Go out in sunlight, end it all

It's not that easy to take your own life
When the music of murder does call.

As I'm drinking your blood and ending your dayS
Part of me is instantly filled
And though it is evil when I see your frozen gaze
I'm proud of that effortless kill.

There's beauty in moonlight that goes on forever
Lighting gardens filled with blood red roses
In the shadows the moon's lighting paths to wherever
And sillouette trees strike macabre poses.

I'm forced back to my prison, silk lined and cold
As on with your life you go
Only memories I have to hold
As forevermore I grow more old.

Poor Johnny McGee

Poor Johnny McGee
Poor Johnny McGee
He fell for me and broke his knee
Poor Johnny McGee.

Poor Johnny McGee
Poor Johnny McGee
Fell down a well and went straight to Hell
Poor Johnny McGee.

Poor Johnny McGee
Poor Johnny McGee
Fell down the stairs and found no one cares
Poor Johnny McGee.

Poor Johnny McGee
Poor Johnny McGee
Liked at a hot pie and burnt his eye
Poor Johnny McGee.

Poor Johnny McGee
Poor Johnny McGee
Tried to lift a wheel and smashed his heel
Poor Johnny McGee.

Poor Johnny McGee
Poor Johnny McGee
Now the poem's at its end about my very special
friend
Poor Johnny McGee.

I Hate Hospitals

I hate hospitals
I really do
I'm only here because of you.
I hate the wards
With plain walls
I'm only here because of that call.
I hate the sounds
The ceaseless beep beep
That goes on and on while you sleep.
I hate the sights
That antiseptic smell
I'm only here praying you will get well.

Haunted House

There's a haunted house at the end of my street
Where the windows bang and hinges squeak.
I see an old man who still lives there
He's got big black boots and fading grey hair.

The garden's overgrown, well it's a mess
I almost got lost there when I looked for old
Tess.
During the day it's frightening alright
But no one goes near when the day turns to
night.

The old man's so pale, he's white as a sheet
That old man who lives at the bottom of my
street.
From the attic the old man spies
Though no one really knows if he has eyes.

"He's a ghost" the kids at my school cry
"I've seen him hovering in the sky"
I've never seen him flying yet
Or stealing children in his big fishing net.

But the naughty children are all gone
There's only a sad little old school song

From the old scary house at the end of my road
With its gate that groans like a big fat toad.

If there's a haunted house at the end of your
street
Don't be a bully, keep your bedroom neat
Because another old man might just live there
With big black boots and fading grey hair.

If I Were A Princess

If I were a Princess in a fairytale
On a magnificent ship I'd sail
To visit a kingdom across the sea
Where you my Prince would wait for me.

If I were a Princess in a beautiful palace I would live
And to my people a smile I'd give
I'd be kind to all people until the end
When for me my Prince would send.

If I were a Princess a Queen someday I'd be
With you as my King standing beside me
Together we'd rule and be just and fair
And our kingdom would never have a care.

But I'm not a Princess in a children's story
And your not a Prince all draped in glory
But that doesn't matter at all you see
I'm anything I want because you love me.

Blackie

I've got a cat, Blackie is her name
And pouncing on my brother is her favourite
game.
Her face, ears and body are all black
Just like she fell in a coal man's sack.

She's not like other cats who curl up by the fire
Or jump up trees she walks around and can't
climb higher.
I've had from a kitten for so long now
And it's a comforting sound to hear her purr and
miaow.

When she sleeps it's on my bed
With her black tail like a pillow for her black
head
Blackie's not just a cat or a pet you see
She's the youngest member of my family.

www.ingramcontent.com/pod-product-compliance
Lightning Source LLC
Chambersburg PA
CBHW062110140826
49812CB00058B/1156
9789395784436